How to Make a Charcuterie Board

Easy and Super Fun to Make for Family

Copyright © 2020

All rights reserved.

DEDICATION

The author and publisher have provided this e-book to you for your personal use only. You may not make this e-book publicly available in any way. Copyright infringement is against the law. If you believe the copy of this e-book you are reading infringes on the author's copyright, please notify the publisher at: https://us.macmillan.com/piracy

Contents

Recipe 1 1

Recipe 2 9

Recipe 3 23

Recipe 4 42

Recipe 1

Charcuterie boards are not only gorgeous, they contain a combination of flavors and nibbles for a simple no-fuss party snack!

It's not difficult to prepare a meat and cheese board that everyone will rave about! Adding various flavors from simple everyday ingredients takes very little prep and just minutes to build!

I've included a few tips below to make sure your next party platter is the talk of the event!

First off ... how do you pronounce charcuterie? [shahr-koo-tuh–ree].

Charcuterie is the art of preparing meats which are often cured or smoked such as bacon, ham or salami. A charcutier is a person who prepares charcuterie and while the term is loosely translated in English to "pork butcher", any kind of meat can be used.

A charcuterie board is commonly seen on menus pretty much

everywhere these days and it's the perfect way to enjoy some nibbles with friends and family!

Preparing a Charcuterie Board

A charcuterie board most often consists of a variety of meats and cheeses and often fruit or nuts; essentially a meat and cheese board!

It's very easy to prepare a charcuterie and you can find absolutely everything you need at Walmart!

The gorgeous wood board in the photos on this post was purchased at Walmart (it's a part of the Pioneer Woman Collection) along with all of the ingredients! If you'd prefer, Walmart also has a great selection of plates to create the perfect Charcuterie platter!

As you begin thinking about making the perfect charcuterie board, you will want to start thinking about different colors and textures to make it vibrant and interesting.

Red and black berries, dried apricots, fresh herbs, pickles, olives and various dips can add lots of color.

The board should look full, don't be afraid to pile and stack them while thinking about varying the different items throughout.

Meat: I estimate about 3-4 slices of meat per person when building a board. I try to include a variety of flavors and textures for example a sliced pepper salami, a rolled prosciutto and thoughtfully piled ham.

Cheese: Choose a variety of cheeses; about 1 or 2 oz per person as an hors d'oeuvre. Look for various hard and soft cheeses from mellow to sharp. Cheeses are easiest served already sliced.

Bread and Crackers: Again variety is key, I like to include buttery flaky crackers, grain crackers and thinly sliced and toasted baguettes.

Fruit & Nuts: Both dried and fresh fruit will add gorgeous color and lots of flavor to your charcuterie board! As you are purchasing fruits, keep a variety of colors in mind for a beautiful board. Nuts should be shelled and salted.

Pickles, Olives and Dips: Adding small bowls filled with dill pickles, olives, jellies, mustards and delicious dips is a great way to add some zip and flavor to your board.

Most of the items can be prepared, washed and/or sliced ahead of time meaning this easy appetizer can take just minutes to prepare.

A beautiful meat and cheese board with various flavors takes very little prep and just minutes to build! I was able to find all of the items I needed at Walmart. Below is the list of some of my favorite additions!

Cheese

Sliced Monterey Jack Cheese

Sliced Cheddar Cheese

El Cortijo Manchego Wedge Cheese

Bel Gioioso Parmesan Cheese Wedge

Meat

Peppered Salame

Salami

Prosciutto

Ham

Fruit

Dried Apricots

Assorted fresh berries

Cherry tomatoes

Grapes

Crackers/Bread

Marketside French Baguette sliced and toasted

Ritz Crackers

Everything Pretzel Crisps

Artisan or Seeded Crackers

Other

Planters Nuts

Marketside Spinach Dip

Marketside Onion Dip

Great Value Black Olives

Mini Dill Pickles

The next time you need an easy and totally fuss free party snack, creating a charcuterie board is not only loved by everyone… it's so pretty!

Recipe 2

I'm a big cheese lover. Growing up, my dad would always snack on slices of cheese with crackers and I'd often join him for this after school treat (he still would rather have cheese & crackers than a real dinner!). I even gave up cheese one year for lent, because that's how much I love it. Ha!

These days I don't really eat very much cheese in my everyday diet, but I do indulge in it when we're hosting friends & family (and pizza...duh!). So it shouldn't be a surprise that my go-to party dish is a simple charcuterie board.

How to Make a Charcuterie Board

Whenever we have people over, I always have a charcuterie board filled with various cheese, meats, nuts, and crackers. I love this appetizer because there is zero real cooking involved (you guys know my limits in the kitchen), and if you do it the right way your charcuterie board can act as decor during your little shindig! I mean how gorgeous & vibrant is this setup?!

How to Make a Charcuterie Board

INGREDIENTS

Soft Cheese: I usually go with a brie

Mild Cheese: Gouda every.single.time.

Firm: Unexpected Cheddar

Prosciutto/various meats

Nuts

Fruit

Olives

Crackers

Dried Fruit

Veggies

Hummus

INSTRUCTIONS

Start by cutting up all the cheese. Keep the pieces bite-sized to best fit on the board. For the brie (or other soft cheeses), just put the wedge on the board and include a cheese knife (love this set) so guests can slice off their own.

Next, add the meat. Meats like prosciutto, salami, or turkey are popular. You can use what you prefer, and what your guests will like!

Add the light sides next, like a selection of olives, veggies for dipping, and hummus. Serve these sides in small ramekins to keep them from making a mess!

Next, add the snacks. Fresh fruit and dried fruit like grapes, raspberries, strawberries, raisins, dried cranberries, and dried apricots add color to the board.

Crackers come next. I used raisin rosemary crisps and multigrain pita chips. Other popular options are pretzel chips,

Ritz crackers, or saltines. There are many options to include!

Fill in the gaps between the main features with small additions like nuts. My favorites are almonds, candied pecans, and pistachios.

Arrange your board however you think looks appetizing and presentable! Include your favorite treats and a great variety of options for all your guests.

Simple Charcuterie Board – Ingredients

Soft Cheese: I usually go with a brie, just be sure to keep a cheese knife out for your guests.

Mild Cheese: Gouda every.single.time.

Firm: Unexpected Cheddar (this is from Trader Joe's and it's delicious. Crumbly, hard, and tangy!)

Prosciutto/various meats

Nuts

How to Make a Charcuterie Board

Fruit

Olives

Crackers

Dried Fruit

Veggies

Hummus

Finding the Perfect Wood Board

You first need a large wood board to hold all your goodies. I have this round wooden board (super old from Crate & Barrel) that I use for all of my charcuterie plates, but I'd love to invest in a few more. I always go with a round shape, but rectangles work well too. Here are some of my favorites…

If you have a lot of snacks to serve, consider doing a round platter as your main area and a long rectangular board for overflow!

Charcuterie Board Tips

How to Make a Charcuterie Board

The first thing I do is cut up the cheese. I just use a regular knife, but I've heard cheese slicers make this task especially easy. I try to keep bites pretty small, so guests can try the cheese with all of the various offerings on the platter.

I always cut the cheese up ahead of time and put them in small tupperware containers. Then when it's time to throw together the charcuterie board (about 15 minutes before guests arrive), I can take the cheese from the fridge and start building my board.

For the brie (or other soft cheeses), just put the wedge on the board and include a cheese knife (love this set) so guests can slice off their own. If I'm having a lot of guests over and may not have time to cut up more cheese, I'll sometimes put the big chunks of harder cheese next to their little slices so guests can cut more if the cubes run out!

I put my 3 cheese on the board in 3 different areas, and then I add the meat. I don't eat red meat or pork, so this category is foreign to me. But you gotta please the people, so I always try to include meat on my boards. Trader Joe's has a good selection of prosciutto and salami that I'll often buy.

With the hearty dishes on the board, I add a little cup of olives. I put these in a ramekin (love these from Crate & Barrel) so they don't leak all over the rest of the snacks. If I also have veggies for dipping, I'll put hummus in a ramekin on the board too.

The Finishing Touches

With the cheeses, meats, and olives on my simple charcuterie board, it's time for the fun stuff....the snacks! I love using fresh fruit & dried fruit to add some color to the board. My go-to is always grapes and I keep them on the vine and plop them right in the center of the board.

Then I'll add berries if I have them, and some sort of dried fruit. This time it was dried apricots.

I love the selection of crackers at Trader Joe's. On here I have my favorite Raisin Rosemary Crisps, as well as these Multigrain Pita Bit Crackers. I like to offer a couple kinds of crackers because some pair better with particular cheeses.

Fill in the Gaps

I think a charcuterie board looks best when the plate is full and items are touching. So I usually finish things off by putting nuts in the open areas. On this board, I did both sweet & savory nuts. I have candied pecans, pistachios, and my absolute favorite almonds (these Marcona Almonds with Rosemary from Trader Joe's).

If I have any extra herbs (like rosemary), I'll also scatter those throughout the board for extra color and fragrance. An easy appetizer for Thanksgiving...this simple charcuterie board

And that's pretty much it! Anyone else feeling hungry?! Of course, my charcuterie boards are always changing depending on what we have in the fridge and pantry. But this is my go-to way to bring it all together for a delicious and aesthetically pleasing look!.

This is such an easy no-cook appetizer or snack for the holidays. I hope you'll try to build your own simple charcuterie board for Thanksgiving or a holiday party this year!

Recipe 3

Making a meat + cheese board is like a "choose your own adventure book". You get to pick whatever items you want within 5 categories.

My board featured soft Saint Andre and creamy, tangy gorgonzola, as well as French cheeses like Basque and Comte (my French friend is really having an influence on my cheese selection!). I added delicious cracker breadsticks and raisin rosemary crisps along with blackberry jam, honey with honeycomb and delicious fruits gifted to me from Melissa's Produce that included blood oranges, asian pears and pomegranates.

My hope is that what you take away from this post is a template to make your own board and not a recipe. Don't worry how all the flavors will match together…if each item is something you enjoy, they'll all work beautifully. Trust me!

The Cheeses

You want to choose a variety of cheeses (at least one from each category):

1 soft/semi-soft cheese (brie, goat cheese, gorgonzola, saint andre etc)

1 medium hard (gouda, gruyere, basque etc)

1 hard cheese (comte, raclette)

How to Make a Charcuterie Board

I chose these four cheeses for my board:

Saint Andre (soft)

Gorgonzola (soft)

Basque (medium)

Comte (hard)

The Meats

Choose cured meats in a 2:1 ratio from the cheeses. So for every two cheeses, choose one cured meat. This isn't a hard and fast rule, by any means, just something for you to think about when you're at the grocery store picking items out.

I chose these two meats for my board:

Prosciutto

Calabrese

The Crackers

Choose 2-3 different types of crackers for your board. I like to choose crackers that are either easy to dip with or sturdy enough to spread cheese onto. Other than that, you can do anything you'd like.

For my board I chose:

Trader Joe's Italian Breadstick crackers

Trader Joe's Raisin Rosemary Crisps

Dips/Spreads

Choose your own adventure when it comes to dips and spreads! There are so many items to choose from these days that you don't have to make yourself.

Dips/Spreads

Pate, jams/jellies, pepper jelly, honey, tapenade, hummus etc.

For my board I chose:

Blackberry jam

Honey with honeycomb

Truffle honey

The Fillers/Fun Stuff

Fillers can be any assortment of these items:

Salted nuts that aren't too small

Pecans, pistachios, cashews, rosemary or truffle almonds

Dried fruits

Montmorency cherries, mangoes, raisins, orange slices, pineapple rings

Fresh fruits

Apples, pears, oranges, pomegranates, grapes (the list goes on!)

Other sweets

Dark chocolate covered almonds, yogurt coated pretzels, nougat etc.

For my board I chose:

Dried Montmorency cherries

Salted/Roasted Pecan halves

Blood oranges

Pomegranates

Butterscotch Asian Pears

How to Make a Charcuterie Board

Step 1: Arrange Cheeses

Arrange the cheeses, evenly spaced onto the board. Half crumble the cheeses that will crumble and slice the cheeses that are medium to hard types.

Step 2: Place Meat Next to Cheeses

Arrange the sliced meats right next to the cheeses. Fold them nicely to add texture to the board.

How to Make a Charcuterie Board

Step 3: Add Crackers Next to Meats

Shingle the crackers next to the meats.

Step 4: Add Dips/Spreads

Place small containers of the dips and spreads onto the board. You can use small metal or glass containers. For a shortcut, buy containers of dip/spreads that are already small so you don't have to portion them into something else.

How to Make a Charcuterie Board

Step 5: Add Fillers/Fun Stuff

Sprinkle all the "fillers" into the empty spaces like nuts, dried fruit, fresh fruit. The goal is to fill any empty space at all. Just make sure any hard fruits like pears or apples are sliced very thin.

Step 6: Garnish w/ Herbs (optional)

Stick beautiful pieces of greenery around the board evenly like rosemary, thyme, edible flowers (if you want to get really fancy!).

There you have it!

A simple step-by-step DIY charcuterie board that is perfect for Valentine's day with your honey or a get together with friends.

But how much should I make?

Chef's tip: Honestly, use your best judgement, but a little goes a long way and people do tend to moderate themselves based on the amount of food presented to them. When it's gone, it's gone! This is only an appetizer-like dish so you don't need a lot.

Print

How to Make a Charcuterie Board

DIY Easy Charcuterie Board

a template (not a recipe) to build your own meat + cheese board

Course Appetizer

Keyword charcuterie board, meat and cheese board

Ingredients

Cheeses

1 small block Saint Andre w/ cheese knife stuck into it

1 small block gorgonzola half crumbled and cheese knife stuck into it

1 small block Basque cheese sliced thin

1 small block Comte sliced thin

Meats

1 package prosciutto folded

1 package Calabrese salami folded

Crackers

1 box Trader Joe's Italian breadstick crackers

How to Make a Charcuterie Board

1 box Trader Joe's raisin rosemary crackers

Dips/Spreads

blackberry jam

honey with honeycomb

Fillers/Fun Stuff

1 pomegrante tendrils

1 asian pear sliced thin

1 blood orange sliced thin

salted roasted pecan halves

dried Montmorency cherries

Garnishes

a few rosemary sprigs

Instructions

Add the cheeses onto the board evenly.

Add the sliced meats next to the cheeses.

Add the crackers next to the meats.

Add the dips/spreads in small containers evenly spaced onto the board (into a triangle formation is best visually).

Next, add the "fillers" and fill any and all empty spaces!

Tuck in any garnish if using. Ta da!

As guests eat items from the board, fill in empty spots with leftover meats, cheeses etc.

Recipe 4

How to make a crowd-pleasing charcuterie board, complete with cheese and meat selections, wine pairings, and suggestions for incorporating seasonal ingredients to make a winning wine and cheese board any time of year!

How to Make a Charcuterie Board

Appetizers — they're the new dinner party.

I've noticed tapas and appetizers (or apps as my friends call them) have become the new To Do for get-togethers.

It used to be, my friends and I would throw some burgers on the grill and crack open some cheap beers, but now that we're getting older, we're all about doing the sophisticated things.

Things like meeting up for a glass of wine and an appetizer at a cool local bar or pairing food and alcohol with a small group in one of our backyards, complete with the musical stylings of Snoop Dogg Pandora Radio.

Being the person in charge of appetizers can sometimes be stressful since you never know what your friends are in the mood for, which is where the charcuterie board comes into play.

What is a Charcuterie Board?

Ahhh, the charcuterie board. The board that is full of mystery, variety, explosions of flavor ... the board that everyone (including myself) has trouble pronouncing.

In case you're unfamiliar, charcuterie (prounounced shar-kood-eree) boards are meat and cheese boards that typically include a variety of items that can be paired in mouth-watering combinations.

They usually include various ingredients that complement the meats and cheeses for a fun do-it-yourself appetizer experience for your guests.

I love charcuterie boards because they can please just about any palate, and your guests can whip up all sorts of combinations to keep their experience unique and entertaining. Plus, they can be actioned any time of year, using seasonal eats.

How to Make a Charcuterie Board

During the summer months is when most of us do the majority of our entertaining, and charcuterie boards are brilliant for pleasing any crowd, while taking some of the workload off your shoulders.

We don't need to turn on the oven or hover over the stove top or spend a great deal of time cooking. All we do is add arrange a variety of ingredients to a large serving board with crackers and/or bread and let our guests loose. This no-bake appetizer extravaganza keeps your friends and family satisfied until the main course comes around.

While putting together a charcuterie board may seem overwhelming at first glance, it's actually quite easy and enjoyable.

I have all sorts of tips for putting together the ultimate charcuterie board that doesn't require a huge investment or a special butcher or market . So let's dive in, starting with some basic tips.

How to Make a Charcuterie Board:

Select a variety of meat and cheese, meaning an assortment of mild, medium and bold flavors. Some people prefer softer, mild meats and cheeses, where other folks love big, bold flavors. Be sure you have options for both mild and bold flavors, as well as middle-of-the-road options.

Add seasonal fruit to the mix. While the main event attraction of a charcuterie board should be the meat, it is always smart to include fresh in-season fruit to add sweetness to the salty and to change up the experience. If you want to get extra fancy, you can roast or grill fresh fruit.

Jams or preserves: Include 1 or 2 jams or preserves for some added flavor and sweetness to balance out the dry and salty meat and cheese. Fig spread goes marvelously with many cheeses and meats, so I always like to include it. I also like to include apricot jam, but raspberry or grape jam works, too. Again, you can step this up by using homemade jams, but store-bought works great and chances are you already have several options in your pantry.

Provide something briny to pair with the meat and cheese. Pickled vegetables, such as gherkins or pickles, olives, pickled jalapenos or pepperoncinis are great on charcuterie boards. They can be paired easily with the bold meats, such as salami or sopressata, and add a mouth-watering tang.

Other spreads: You may also include any of your favorite spreads, such as stone ground mustard, tapenade, pate, hummus, and/or white bean dip. These spreads are great for smearing on sliced baguette for stacking meat and cheese on top.

Etc.: Get creative by including anything else you think your friends would enjoy. For instance, cheese or chocolate fondue with fresh fruit and bread for dipping, dark chocolate bars, roasted or raw nuts, compound butters, nut butters or hazelnut spread, etc, etc.

Alcohol: When appropriate, include alcohol to your charcuterie experience. Wine and beer pair excellently with meat and cheese and can enhance the flavor experience. Generally speaking, you want to pair bold-flavored meat and cheese with bold-flavored alcohol. For instance, goat cheese, smoked salmon and prosciutto pairs well with white wine, while salami, cheddar and blue cheese go great with red wine.

Crackers & bread: While your guests can get along perfectly well without crackers or sliced baguette, these items can be great for pairing a variety of ingredients for providing stability to the bite. I like to provide gluten-free crackers as well as regular crackers. I choose crackers that don't have a huge amount of flavor, added herbs or salt so that the crackers don't detract from the flavor of what's being added to them.

The finished product: Putting all of these elements together, you will end up with a board that has a variety of pairing options. Here is what I included on the board pictured in this post:

My Favorite Charcuterie Meat & Cheese Selections:

For the meat, I chose prosciutto, pancetta, sopressata, and Genoa salami.

For the cheese: goat chevre, Gruyere, English blue cheese. In the fruit department, I added fresh red grapes, figs, blueberries and dates.

For the spreads, I used a fig spread and apricot preserves, both of which I already had on-hand. Last, but not least, my

briney elements were brown mustard and olives. I also had a

variety of white and red wines, as well as beer available in the refrigerator for whoever wanted it.

Most grocery stores have a deli section with a complete selection of aged meats and cheeses. Even if you don't have a huge bank of knowledge on various meat and cheese pairings, selecting several quality meats and cheeses is key to a fun board.

I picked up a few packages of prosciutto, pancetta, sopressata and Genoa salami, which came pre-sliced. Easy peasy. Generally, aged meats are my go-to over other sliced deli meat because they're full of flavor and tend to be very easy to pair with most cheeses and spreads.

In this way, you don't need to go to the butcher, an expensive natural food store or own a meat slicer — simply use what's already in the deli.

Let's talk cheese:

I typically select at least three cheeses: a mild, medium and sharp cheese. I like to provide at least one non-dairy option, such as sheep milk or goat milk cheese. Goat chevre is my go-to mild cheese and seems to always be a favorite among my friends.

For my medium-bodied cheese, I go for a cheese that will pair well with both white and red wine and most beers: Gruyere or Gouda.

How to Make a Charcuterie Board

And finally, I always bring a blue cheese (but on the mild end of the blues, nothing too blue-y or sharp) since it pairs so well with bold meats and heavy red wines.

Before your friends begin digging in, take a quick minute to explain to them what everything is. Just a general run down of what everything is called is helpful to take a little bit of the guesswork out of making selections. Your friends will have a blast figuring out what flavors they like best together.

For this round of charcuterie-ing, my favorite combo was goat cheese, prosciutto and fig spread on top of a cracker, followed by a sip of white wine.

Great food, great company — what more could you need for a pleasant evening? One of my favorite parts about getting friends together to enjoy a charcuterie board is we all inevitably end up discussing our favorite profiles. Simple conversations like these are sometimes the most relaxing and memorable.

And that is all, folks. As my high school math teacher would say, "Nothing to it but to do it." What are your favorite charcuterie-ables?

How to make a charcuterie board with cheese, meat, nuts, fruit, spreads, etc.

INGREDIENTS

MEAT & CHEESE:

How to Make a Charcuterie Board

10 to 12 oz soft cheeses of choice blue cheese, brie cheese, goat cheese, marinated feta etc.

10 to 12 oz aged cheeses of choice parmesan, Gouda, Gruyere, aged cheddar, etc.

10 to 12 oz cured meat prosciutto, pancetta, roast beef, turkey deli meat, black forest ham, etc.

SPREADS:

10 to 12 oz spreads of choice tapenade, pate, mustard, hummus, fig preserves, jam, jelly

NUTS, DRIED FRUIT, FRESH FRUIT:

2 cups nuts of choice raw or roasted almonds, pecans, walnuts

1 to 2 cups dried fruit of choice dried cranberries, figs, dates, etc.

2 to 3 lbs fresh fruit grapes, peaches, apples, blueberries, strawberries ETC.

4 oz dark chocolate

CRACKERS/BREAD

1 large baguette toasted and sliced

How to Make a Charcuterie Board

1 to 2 boxes crackers of choice gluten-free, nut and seed crackers, etc.

INSTRUCTIONS

Arrange the meat and cheese on a large cutting board with knives for slicing the cheese and/or meat. Fill in the board with your spreads of choice, fresh fruit, dried fruit, nuts, jams, dark chocolate, etc.

Serve with choice of wine pairings and/or alcoholic or non-alcoholic beverages of choice!

Made in the USA
Middletown, DE
12 December 2021